Diet and Obesity

Jim Kerr

W
FRANKLIN WATTS
LONDON•SYDNEY

First published in 2008
by Franklin Watts

Copyright © Franklin Watts 2008

Franklin Watts
338 Euston Road
London NW1 3BH

Franklin Watts Australia
Level 17/207 Kent Street
Sydney, NSW 2000

Editor: Jeremy Smith
Design: Simon Borrough
Art director: Jonathan Hair
Picture research: Diana Morris

Picture credits: AJ Photo/Science Photo Library: 40. Brian Bell/Science Photo Library: 41. Vince Bevan/Alamy: 26. Tim Boyle/Getty Images: 24. BSIP, Laurent/Science Photo Library: 32bl. David Cantrille/Alamy: 18. Matt Cardy/Getty Images: 8. digieye/Shutterstock: front cover t. Emilio Ereza/Alamy: front cover b. Najiah Feanny/Corbis: 25. Jon Feingersch/zefa/Corbis: 14. Mauro Fermariello/ Science Photo Library: 35. The Gallery Collection/Corbis: 11. Eric Gevaert/Shutterstock: 29r. Bob Handelman/Alamy: 6. Tom Henley/Alamy: 23. istockphoto: 31. Ann Johansson/Corbis: 12. Karen Kasmauski/Corbis: 13, 21. Graham Lawrence/Alamy: 28. Veronique Leplar/Science Photo Library: 30. Martin Luther King Junior School: 36. Alan Novelli/ Alamy: back cover. Oak Ridge National Lab/US Dept of Energy/Science Photo Library: 16. Cristina Pedrazzini/ Science Photo Library: 32br. PNC/zefa/Corbis: 17. John Powell/ Rex Features: 33t. Ross Ressmeyer/Corbis: 15. Reuters/Corbis: 34. Michael Reynolds/epa/Corbis: 20. Rex Features: 33b. Rick Rycroft/AP: 39. Alex Segre/Alamy: 19. Ian Shaw/Alamy: 37t, 37b. The Simpsons tm © Fox & its related companies. All Rights Reserved: 10. Lucy Tizard /Alamy: 27. Ahmad Yusni/epa/Corbis: 29l.

A CIP catalogue record for this book
is available from the British Library.

Dewey number: 629.47

ISBN 978 0 7496 8102 9

Printed in China

Franklin Watts is a division of Hachette Children's Books,
an Hachette Livre UK company.
www.hachettelivre.co.uk

Contents

What is obesity?

People are considered to be obese when they are carrying too much body fat for their height and sex. According to the World Health Organization (WHO), obesity is a condition that can affect all groups of people – young and old, male and female, rich and poor. The number of obese people worldwide is rising fast, making obesity the biggest health problem faced by many countries.

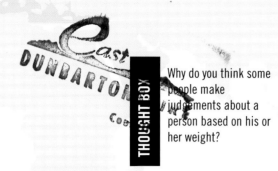

THOUGHT BOX

Why do you think some people make judgements about a person based on his or her weight?

Obesity and health

Obesity causes a number of health problems. It can lead to serious illnesses including heart disease, cancer, diabetes, arthritis and kidney disease. Some of these shorten life expectancy, others affect people's quality of life. In addition, the obese body shape is considered to be unattractive in many parts of the world. As a result, many obese people lack confidence and suffer low self-esteem.

Piling on the weight

People do not become obese overnight. Gradually they gain weight as they continue to eat more food than their body needs. Obese people often eat a poor diet – eating too many foods that are high in fat but which do not satisfy hunger – while leading a lifestyle that is low in physical activity. A few obese people have an illness or a genetic reason for being obese.

Measuring obesity

Obesity can be measured in a number of different ways. The most common measure is Body Mass Index (BMI). This is a person's weight in kilograms divided by their height in metres squared (kg/m^2). Obesity is also calculated by waist-to-hip ratio, which divides the circumference of a person's waist by their hips and it is measured by the percentage of body fat.

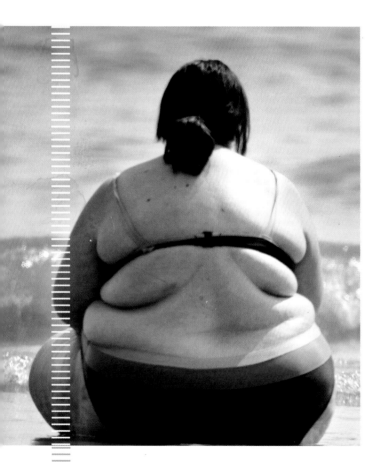

The main causes of obesity are bad choices of diet and declining levels of exercise.

Height (feet and inches)

Weight (pounds) / Weight (kilograms)

lb	5'0"	5'1"	5'2"	5'3"	5'4"	5'5"	5'6"	5'7"	5'8"	5'9"	5'10"	5'11"	5'12"	6'1"	6'2"	6'3"	6'4"	kg
100	20	19	18	18	17	17	16	16	15	15	14	14	14	13	13	12	12	45
105	21	20	19	19	18	17	17	16	16	16	15	15	14	14	13	13	13	47
110	21	21	20	19	19	18	18	17	17	16	16	15	15	15	14	14	13	50
115	22	22	21	20	20	19	19	18	17	17	17	16	16	15	15	14	14	52
120	23	23	22	21	21	20	19	19	18	18	17	17	16	16	15	15	15	54
125	24	24	23	22	21	21	20	19	19	18	18	17	17	16	16	16	15	57
130	25	25	24	23	22	22	21	20	20	19	19	18	18	17	17	16	16	59
135	26	26	25	24	23	22	22	22	21	21	20	19	19	18	18	17	17	61
140	27	26	26	25	24	23	23	22	21	21	20	20	19	18	18	17	17	63
145	28	27	27	26	25	24	23	23	22	21	21	20	20	19	19	18	18	66
150	29	28	27	27	26	25	24	23	23	22	22	21	20	20	19	19	18	68
155	30	29	28	27	27	26	25	24	24	23	22	22	21	20	20	19	19	70
160	31	30	29	28	27	27	26	25	24	24	23	22	22	21	21	20	19	72
165	32	31	30	29	28	27	27	26	25	24	24	23	22	22	21	21	20	75
170	33	32	31	30	29	28	27	27	26	25	24	23	23	22	22	21	21	77
175	34	33	32	31	30	29	28	27	27	26	25	24	24	23	22	22	21	79
180	35	34	33	32	31	30	29	28	27	27	26	25	24	24	23	22	22	82
185	36	35	34	33	32	31	30	29	28	27	27	26	25	24	24	23	23	84
190	37	36	35	34	33	32	31	30	29	28	27	26	26	25	24	24	23	86
195	38	37	36	35	33	32	31	31	30	29	28	27	26	26	25	24	24	88
200	39	38	37	35	34	33	32	31	30	30	29	28	27	26	26	25	24	91
205	40	39	37	36	35	34	33	32	31	30	29	29	28	27	26	26	25	93
210	41	40	38	37	36	35	34	33	32	31	30	29	29	28	28	27	26	95
215	42	41	39	38	37	36	35	34	33	32	31	30	29	28	28	27	26	98
220	43	42	40	39	38	37	36	34	33	32	32	31	30	29	28	27	27	100
225	44	43	41	40	39	37	36	35	34	33	32	31	31	30	29	28	27	102
230	45	43	42	41	39	38	37	36	35	34	33	32	31	30	30	29	28	104
235	46	44	43	42	40	39	38	37	36	35	34	33	32	31	30	29	29	107
240	47	45	44	43	41	40	39	38	36	35	34	33	33	32	31	30	29	109
245	48	46	45	43	42	41	40	38	37	36	35	34	33	32	31	31	30	111
250	49	47	46	44	43	42	40	39	38	37	36	35	34	33	32	31	30	114

Height (centimetres): 150 152.5 155 157.5 160 162.5 165 167.5 170 172.5 175 177.5 180 182.5 185 187.5 190

Calculate your Body Mass Index using this table. Find your height and your weight measurements on this chart. The box in the middle where these two meet tells you your BMI. A BMI of 20–25 indicates a healthy body weight in relation to size.

A history of obesity

Obesity is an age-old health condition. Attitudes towards overweight people vary — obesity has been appreciated and shunned in different cultures and at different times.

Anti-obese

The Ancient Egyptians thought obesity was a harmful disease, and it features in Egyptian wall-paintings showing various illnesses. The Aztecs of fifteenth century Mexico believed that obesity was a harmful affliction of disapproving gods. In Western European culture, obesity was linked with the biblical sin of gluttony.

In the 1900s, as obesity became more widespread in the developed world, it was seen as unfashionable. This attitude increased as the medical problems associated with obesity became clearer. One of the first charts of ideal weights for various heights was produced in the 1940s. Governments began campaigns targeting obesity, including diet and exercise programmes, and companies began to market diet food products in the 1950s.

In modern Western culture, the obese body shape is seen as unattractive by many people. Negative stereotypes are associated with obesity, the most common being that obese people are 'fat, ugly and lazy'. Obesity is also often seen as a sign of lower status and poverty.

There are plenty of negative images of obese people in popular culture, for example bullies such as Nelson Muntz in The Simpsons. Some experts argue that these reinforce stereotypes, harming the self-esteem of obese people.

Positively plump

In some cultures, obesity has mostly been associated with the positive images of physical attractiveness, strength and fertility. Obesity was considered to be a symbol of wealth and high social status in cultures that suffered food shortages or famine. This view was held until just a few hundred years ago in European cultures. But as food became less scarce, obesity began to be seen as a sign of gross appetite.

In some parts of the world, including African, Arabic, Indian and Pacific Island cultures, people are more accepting of obesity. In areas where food continues to be scarce, obesity is seen as a symbol of wealth and high status. For example, before a wedding, brides in certain African tribes are pampered to gain weight until they reach a suitable size.

THOUGHT BOX

Why do you think that members of the 'fat acceptance' movement feel the need to promote positive images of obesity, defend the rights of obese people and prevent their social exclusion?

The plump or fleshy models painted by Rubens (1577–1640) were considered at the time to be the most attractive of women. To this day, curvaceous women are often described as 'Rubenesque'.

'The devil has put a penalty on **all things we enjoy** in life. Either we suffer in health or we suffer in soul or we get fat.' **Albert Einstein (1879–1955)**

The obesity epidemic

According to the WHO, the world's population contained approximately 1.6 billion overweight adults in 2005. At least 400 million of these people were obese – and the WHO think this figure will rise to around 700 million by 2015.

The scale of the problem

The obesity crisis is so serious that the WHO has set up an International Obesity Task Force to tackle the problem. Individual governments have their own teams working on projects to prevent obesity, improve awareness of the problem and help those who are already obese.

A healthy weight

Most experts believe that in adults, a BMI of 20–25 indicates a healthy body weight in relation to height. A BMI of more than 25 is termed overweight, and a BMI of more than 30 is considered to be obese. Measuring obesity in children is more difficult because they are still growing. Other things, such as rate of growth, age, sex and the BMI of other children of the same age, must also be considered. It is best for a child or a teenager to consult a doctor for advice as to whether they are overweight although there are many BMI calculator websites available on the Internet.

In some parts of the world, such as the Caribbean, adult obesity rates have almost quadrupled over the last 25 years.

'On an African level we see now that obesity is a really

major disease

in line with HIV and malnutrition. And it is quite clear that malnutrition and obesity can co-exist at the same time and in the same country.'
Professor Arne Astrup, International Association for the Study of Obesity

THOUGHT BOX Can you think why the adoption of the Western diet has contributed to an increase in overweight children in some developing countries?

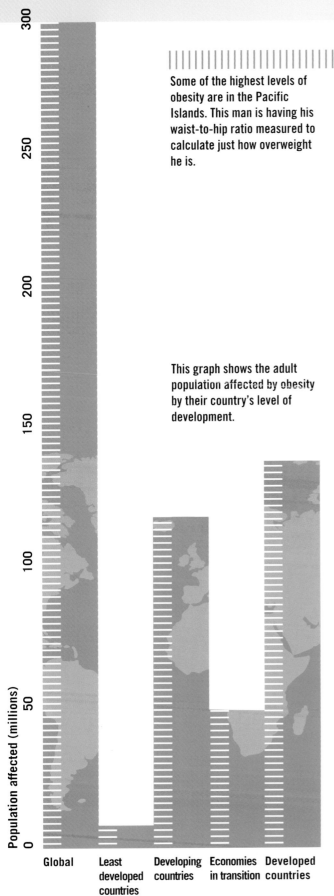

Some of the highest levels of obesity are in the Pacific Islands. This man is having his waist-to-hip ratio measured to calculate just how overweight he is.

This graph shows the adult population affected by obesity by their country's level of development.

Population affected (millions)

300
250
200
150
100
50
0

Global | Least developed countries | Developing countries | Economies in transition | Developed countries

Obesity in developing countries

Obesity is not just a problem in the developed world. It also exists in developing countries, where governments now have the double problem of dealing with malnutrition and obesity in the same population. In fact, rates of obesity are increasing faster in developing countries than in the developed world, especially in towns and cities.

There are variations in rates of obesity across the developed world. According to some statistics, more than 20 per cent of the world's total obese population lives in the USA. Yet, in Japan, another developed country, obesity levels remain below 5 per cent. Australia has seen a rapid rise in rates of obesity, particularly in males, and has some of the fastest-growing levels of childhood obesity.

The causes of obesity

Diet and exercise are the key elements in the debate about obesity. Body weight stays the same when the amount of energy taken in as food equals the amount of energy used by the body. This is called the energy balance. Food energy comes from fat, carbohydrate and protein. When the body doesn't use up all the energy absorbed from food, it is stored as fat. Fat is the body's protection in case of starvation – a rare occurrence in modern life.

The popularity of fast foods and large portions means it is easy to take in more energy than we need.

'The increase in **grazing and snacking** has increased the fat content of our diets. This, coupled with less exercise, means we are beginning to count the cost of these trends.'
Dr Andrew Prentice, Dunn Clinical Nutrition Centre, Cambridge, UK

Energy going in

Scientists calculate that adult men need an average of 2,550 calories, or units of food energy, each day to stay healthy. Adult women need slightly fewer – around 1,940 calories on average. However, most people in the developed world eat far more calories than this.

It is not just the amount of food eaten that is causing people to gain weight, or even become obese, but what they eat. In recent years, there has been an explosion of food with a high fat content, including convenience foods and ready-made meals. Many people eat far more fat in their daily diet than their bodies were designed to cope with. Health experts say there is a strong link between body fat and the fat content of the diet.

Energy going out

The energy in food is used by the body in three ways. About 60 per cent of food energy is used to maintain body tissues, including muscles and organs. It also regulates body temperature. About 10 per cent of the energy in food is lost as body heat following a meal. A further 15 per cent of the food energy is used up by daily life – getting dressed, walking about the house, going to school or work, talking to friends. The final 15 per cent is used in leading an active life – walking to school, playing sport, playing active games or running up the stairs. When someone leads a sedentary life, some of that final 15 per cent of food energy could end up as body fat.

Average daily nutritional and energy needs

Age		Males (kcal)	Females (kcal)
0-3	months	545	515
4-6	months	690	645
7-9	months	825	765
10-12	months	920	865
1-3	years	1230	1165
4-6	years	1715	1545
7-10	years	1970	1740
11-14	years	2220	1845
15-18	years	2755	2110
19-50	years	2550	1940
51-59	years	2550	1900
60-64	years	2380	1900
65-74	years	2330	1900
74+	years	2100	1810

Health experts say that adults should take at least 30 minutes of physical activity at least 3 days during the week.

THOUGHT BOX

Obesity is caused by people overeating in relation to their energy needs. Why do people eat more than their body needs?

A question of genes

The science of genetics studies how tiny units of the body, called genes, pass on information, for example on eye or hair colour, from one generation to the next. There is a great deal of controversy over the issue of whether or not genes affect weight gain. Some research shows that children are more likely to be obese if their parents are obese, but is this due to genetics or family lifestyle?

Passing on the fat

Some rare genetic conditions may be related to obesity, for example Prader-Willi Syndrome, which affects the gene that controls appetite. Scientists have also identified other genes that affect weight gain. But few scientists believe that obesity can be explained solely by genetics because of the huge increase in obesity rates in the past 20 years. During this time there has been no major change in the genes of the world's population.

Monitoring for obesity

Some experts argue that screening for genes that might play a part in obesity could help to identify children at risk of becoming overweight. Measures could then be taken to help this group control their body weight.

Scientists are constantly searching for genes that may cause us to become overweight. One of the mice below has an obesity gene that has caused it to balloon in size.

'We're spending energy by **fidgeting**, and this is one of the key factors in energy balance. People who fidget are more protected against diet-induced obesity, for example, than people who are more calm.'

Professor Mathias Treier, a member of a group of scientists working in Germany and the United says if your genes cause you to fidget, **you are less likely to be fat.**

Family diet

Whether or not there is a genetic factor, parents can pass a tendency to gain weight on to their children by establishing poor eating habits in childhood. If children grow up to enjoy a diet rich in fat and sugar, they will probably continue to eat these foods in adulthood. Even if they don't put on weight in childhood, the sedentary lifestyle of most adults will see the overload of calories in their fat-laden diet turn into weight gain.

Family lifestyle

Children can also 'inherit' an active, or a sedentary, lifestyle from their parents. Children who enjoy an active lifestyle in childhood are more likely to remain a healthy weight. Conversely, families that stay inside a lot, watch television and play computer games for hours establish poor lifestyle habits in their children.

This family's sedentary lifestyle has meant that all of its members have become overweight.

Does modern life cause obesity?

Studies show that in many countries people use up less energy in their daily lives than was the case in the recent past. This is thought to be one of the main causes of the obesity epidemic. Comfortable homes with labour-saving devices and the latest in-house entertainment systems are a feature of modern life in many parts of the world. Many more adults work in offices, rather than in building work, farming or other occupations that use up a lot more energy.

Car culture

One of the biggest changes in lifestyle during the past 50 years explains why levels of exercise are falling. Travel by car has replaced walking and cycling. While people used to regularly walk to work and school, even if it was quite a distance, now people hop in their cars. More and more people can afford to own cars worldwide, which has the knock-on effect of making the streets increasingly unpleasant for the remaining cyclists and pedestrians.

Better by bike

In certain countries, such as the Netherlands, Finland and Denmark, a much slower increase in obesity has occurred in the last 20 years. Some people point out that this can be partly explained by a good approach to eating, especially for children. However, it also seems that active lifestyles, especially walking and cycling (left), are more widespread in these nations.

Cycling rates versus levels of obesity
Prevalence of overweight children aged about 10 years.

UK   Sweden   Germany   Switzerland   Denmark

UK   Sweden   Germany   Switzerland   Denmark

Levels of cycling for 10-year-olds in selected countries

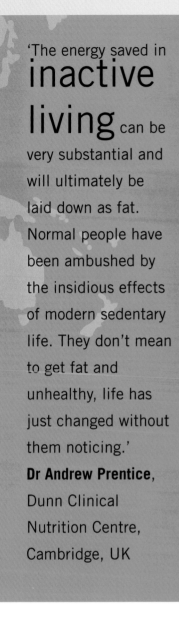
Office culture

Many office workers are at risk of gaining weight, even if they do not exceed average calorie intake, because their lives are so sedentary. An office worker who parks his car outside work and does not take any daily exercise may need only about 1,500 calories a day, while a man working on a building site may use up as many as 4,000–5,000 calories a day. It is very easy to eat more than 1,500 calories in a normal Western diet.

View from the couch

People now choose to spend their leisure time in less physical activities. For example, TV viewing has doubled in the UK since the 1960s, when the average person watched television for 13 hours a week. In some nations, statistics show that outdoor play by young people has reduced. Children often choose to watch television or play on computer games rather than play outdoors or join in with sporting activities. This may be partly due to increased car traffic making streets unsafe for play and a common concern amongst modern parents that it is no longer safe to allow children to play in the park unattended.

Once they have arrived at work, office workers spend most of their days at their desks, doing very little exercise.

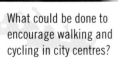

What could be done to encourage walking and cycling in city centres?

THOUGHT BOX

The health costs of obesity

Health experts say that being obese can take nine years off someone's lifespan. This risk is increased if the obese person is a smoker. Even moderately overweight people are at risk of developing serious diseases linked to obesity.

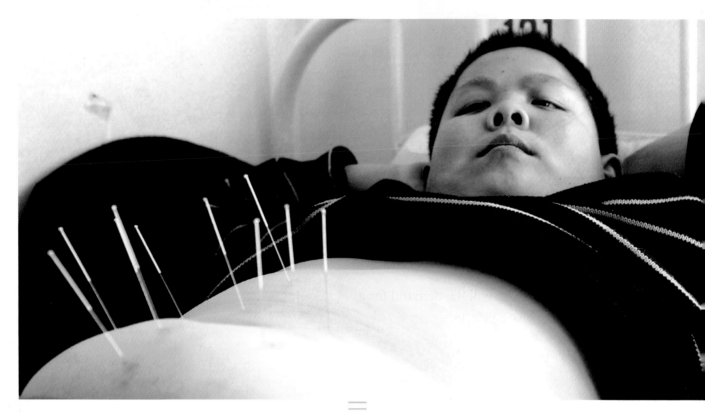

Traditional Chinese medicine uses acupuncture to treat a variety of medical conditions related to childhood obesity.

Obesity and disease

Generalised obesity, which is fat distributed around the whole body, affects the blood circulation and heart. Central obesity, which is fatness mainly around the chest and abdomen, affects the chest and breathing. If someone is obese, they are far more likely to develop diabetes, heart disease, osteoarthritis, high blood pressure, gallstones and certain types of cancers. In addition, they are at risk of being infertile and depressed. More than 9,000 premature deaths a year are caused by obesity in England.

Health predictions

Experts say that, looking at present trends, obesity will soon overtake smoking as the greatest cause of early death. Others claim that children today will be the first generation for over a century for whom life-expectancy will fall. The WHO claims that, over the next 20 years, the number of deaths worldwide as a result of obesity will rise from three million to five million each year.

> 'Obesity is rapidly becoming one of the
> # greatest threats
> to child health.'
> **Dr Vivienne Nathanson**, British Medical Association

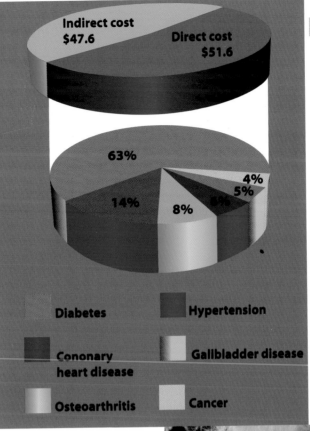

This chart shows the cost of obesity in the USA in 2006, and the types of diseases it can lead to.

- Indirect cost $47.6
- Direct cost $51.6
- 63%
- 14%
- 8%
- 5%
- 4%

Diabetes

Hypertension

Cononary heart disease

Gallbladder disease

Osteoarthritis

Cancer

THOUGHT BOX

According to some experts, childhood obesity affects more than just a student's health. It also increases absences from school. Why do you think that is the case?

Obesity causes problems in children such as diabetes, which can require daily injections to manage.

Healthcare

As levels of obesity rise, so will the demand for a range of medical services. Heart disease, which has reduced as smoking has declined, will begin to rise again. There will be a huge demand for kidney dialysis as obesity increases a person's risk of developing kidney problems. Even simple operations may become more risky as surgeons deal with lower levels of general health and longer operation times caused by dealing with layers of fat in seriously obese patients. Many more clinics for diabetes will be required to help growing numbers of diabetics control their condition.

Childhood obesity

The number of obese children has tripled in the past 20 years. Amongst this group there has been a sharp rise in the number of children developing diabetes. Even those who don't develop diabetes as children are at much greater risk of developing the illness as adults.

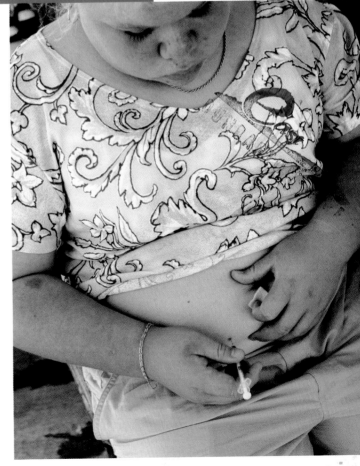

The economic costs of obesity

In many countries, basic healthcare, including doctors' visits, medication and hospital treatment, are paid for by the government and funded by taxation. These governments will need to find extra money to pay for the healthcare of an increasing number of people with obesity. Some experts predict that obesity will cause levels of ill-health that will put great strains on the health services and resources of most countries.

THOUGHT BOX

Reducing obesity will reduce time off work and improve the performance of workers. Should the responsibility for reducing obesity rest with government or employers?

Productivity

Countries rely on a fit and healthy workforce in order to have strong economies. People who have developed serious diseases as a result of their obesity may have long periods of time off work. So, in addition to using up money to treat their condition, they cannot contribute to the production of goods and services that creates wealth.

One report predicts that half of the population of the UK could be obese within the next 25 years. It says that the epidemic will cost the UK economy £45 billion per year by 2050. This shocking number is reached by adding the cost of the loss of productivity from people who suffer health problems caused by obesity to the cost of treating them.

In some countries such as China, regular physical exercise sessions are a part of the daily working routine.

Estimates of the direct costs of obesity

Country	Year of estimate	Proportion of total healthcare expenditure due to obesity	Prevalence of obesity (BMI>30) at time of estimate	latest
USA	2000	4.8%	30.5%	31.5%
Netherlands	1981-89	4.0%	5%	10.3%
Canada	1997	2.4%	14%	13.9%
Portugal	1996	3.5%	11.5%	14%
Australia	1989-90	>2%	10.8%	22%
England	1998	1.5%	19%	23.5%
France	1992	1.5%	6.5%	9%

Fit for work

A large shift towards less physical work has occurred worldwide in the past 50 years. This has reduced physical fat-burning activity in many people's working lives. If the obesity epidemic is to be seriously challenged, employers may need to encourage more daily activity in order to achieve a healthier workforce. For example, they could offer reduced-cost gym membership, or offer interest-free loans or cash incentives to help people buy bicycles that can be used to cycle to work.

'Obesity cost the USA $75bn in 2003. Half this amount – nearly $40bn – came out of public taxes. Researchers say they are alarmed by the growing costs of obesity – both to America's economy and to the health of its people.'

BBC news report on a study by the US Center for Disease Control and Prevention

The misery of obesity

It's hard not to watch the news on television or open a newspaper without hearing the latest grim predictions on the global obesity problem. People who are already overweight or obese can start to feel under attack.

Slim successful

Western society places a great deal of emphasis on people's personal appearance. It is common for people to feel that being slim is necessary to be successful in life.

The media often focuses on the weight gain or loss of celebrities, rather than on their artistic or sporting achievements. The desire to be slim can lead people to feel very dissatisfied with their body shape, which in turn can lead to diets that often end in weight gain, if they fail.

Social outcasts?

It is clear that many overweight people face a lack of acceptance by society. This can lead to feelings of guilt and isolation. Obese people can feel uncomfortable about joining exercise or fitness classes if they are made to feel embarrassed about their weight. Cinema and theatre seats are rarely big enough to accommodate their size. If obese people stay at home, they will take even less exercise and probably seek out food as comfort.

'I fly Sydney to Perth – five hours – and am totally disadvantaged by some huge person next to me literally flopping over into my seat. Why should I pay the same as them?' **Dr John Tickell** a leading Australian nutritionist and author, urges airlines to charge obese passengers more for their seats. He believes a 'fat tax' would highlight his country's obesity crisis and make commercial sense, as heavier loads increase fuel costs.

Dr Tim Gill, of the Australasian Obesity Society writes: 'It's not fair to single out those people who have a problem, which is already impacting greatly on their life.'

Who do you think is right?

Why is obesity such a problem when we seem to be obsessed with diet and fitness?

THOUGHT BOX

Depression and obesity

Controversy reigns over whether depression causes obesity or the other way round. What is clear is that many obese people suffer from depression and low self-esteem. Once an overweight person is depressed, he or she may well continue to overeat to cope with that depression. Not feeling accepted by people makes it hard to form friendships or join new clubs.

One study in the United States found that the longer a child is overweight, the more he or she is at risk of developing depression and other mental health disorders. Young boys proved especially prone to the dual problem of obesity with depression.

In a number of countries, standard-size funfair rides, airline seats, hospital beds, and even coffins and burial plots, can no longer accommodate some obese people.

Food, glorious food!

There are many factors that encourage people to eat too much and gain weight. Part of the blame lies with the global food industry which ensures that food is available in many parts of the world at a low cost, 24 hours a day, and in bigger portions.

Cheap food

Some experts believe that food overproduction has been a major cause of obesity. The United States currently produces approximately 3,900 calories of food per day for every man, woman and child in the country. This is about one-and-a-half times the average daily need. As supply goes up, production costs per unit go down. This means that food is not only produced in greater quantities but is also cheaper to buy. Some experts believe that we are eating our way through an ever-increasing supply of cheap food.

Price promotions

Most supermarkets market themselves as offering food at low cost. They might offer 50 per cent extra free on one product, or 2-for-1 deals on another. The products chosen for these price promotions are usually biscuits, sweets, crisps, sugary drinks and other processed foods, rather than fruit and vegetables. The food is sold in larger quantities or portion sizes at little extra cost, so it offers more value for money for the shopper. But critics say that this is encouraging many people to overeat as they lack the self-discipline to ration their intake of these high-calorie snacks.

THOUGHT BOX

Do you think the food industry is to blame for the rise in obesity levels? How would you advise the manager of your local supermarket to help people make better choices when they are shopping?

In an effort to attract buyers seeking the best deals, supermarkets often promote 2-for-1 budget deals, which may not be good for the obese.

'If we charge money for every calorie of soft drink and fruit drink that was consumed, people would consume less of it. If we subsidise fruit and vegetable production, people would consume more of it and we would have a healthier diet.'

Professor Barry Popkin, University of North Carolina, USA

Although health experts recommend supermarkets stock more healthy and organic food, some chains fear that this will damage sales.

Feeding consumer demand

Price is the top priority for many shoppers in supermarkets. The food industry argues that, in offering food at low cost, it is simply meeting consumer demand. But in an ideal world, the food industry would encourage people to shop for a balanced diet and healthy food would be offered at the cheapest prices.

Advice versus advertisements

Information and education are the keys to helping people being able to make healthy choices about how much to eat, what to eat and when to eat. But it is clear that many people do not follow even the most basic healthy eating recommendations. Some critics say that health information about diet and nutrition is drowned out by advertising and price promotion campaigns by the food industry. The food industry has far bigger budgets for advertising and marketing products than national governments have for their public information campaigns, so this information is far more available to the general public.

Fast food

Eating behaviour has changed dramatically in the past 50 years, with snacking and eating out becoming much more common in many parts of the world. The huge increase in fast-food restaurants during this time has contributed to these changes.

Why is fast food junk food?

Fast-food products are made with ingredients that achieve a certain flavour or consistency, preserve freshness and are low cost. This is done by the use of additives and processing techniques that alter the natural form of food. Fast food tends to have a high fat content, and is high in sugar, salt and animal products. It is often low in vital vitamins and minerals.

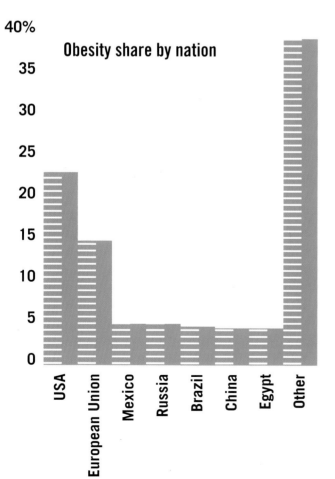

Obesity share by nation

40%

Sweets, snacks and fast food are packed with fat and high levels of sugar and salt. They do not fill you up.

Kids stuff

Some people who are concerned about rising levels of obesity are very critical of advertising campaigns by the food industry that target children. Packaging, give-aways and prominent positions at the end-of-aisle space in supermarkets have been used by the food industry to target young people. Some people claim that food marketing messages have even begun to enter schools. Certain countries, including Sweden and Canada, have taken legal action to limit food marketing to children.

Food marketing — Microstars case study

Free gifts, or give-aways, are a well-used tool for increasing sales by the fast-food chains. One McDonald's campaign called Microstars ran for a five-week period and featured 20 toys to collect in a series. This meant that to collect all the characters for free, a child would need to eat an average of four McDonald's Happy Meals each week. This is well beyond what what be considered healthy by nutritionists.

Cleaning up its act

Some areas of the food industry, after repeated attacks by the media and health experts, have changed some of their products and selling tactics. Certain fast-food chains, including McDonald's, have phased out super-size portions and introduced healthier options. Chocolate bars and biscuit wrappers have started to feature information about eating a balanced diet. Supermarkets have begun to offer more 'deals' on fruit and vegetables, too.

THOUGHT BOX

Do you think that fast-food chains should be doing more to encourage healthy eating?

Global fast-food giant McDonald's operates in more than 119 countries on six continents. McDonald's serves more than 47 million customers around the world each day.

'The decision by McDonald's to introduce healthier foods in its restaurants will not by itself solve the problem of obesity. But they are the market leaders and if it starts a trend and others follow, it could help.' **Dr Toni Steer**, Medical Research Council, UK

Food labelling

In many parts of the world, it is quite common to see the product name, a list of ingredients, a use-by date and storage information on food packaging. Food manufacturers are often required to conform to legal guidelines in each of these areas.

What's in the tin?

Food labelling is key to giving people the information they need to make healthy choices. A clearly understandable system of labels allows shoppers to make informed decisions about what they eat. This helps people to keep track of the calories they are eating, should they wish to do so.

Food standards

Nutritional claims are tightly regulated in many countries. Claims that a product is reduced in fat generally require the food to meet compulsory standards and grades. And in many cases, these claims must be worded in a particular way. Some governments have attempted to tighten regulations on nutrition labelling in response to rising obesity levels. For example, the traffic-light labelling system used in certain countries uses red, amber and green logos to highlight foods that are higher or lower in fat, sugars and salt.

The first place to look for information on what food contains is the nutrition list on the back of the label.

The UK Food Standards Agency traffic light system uses the colours of traffic-light signals to help shoppers choose healthier food at a glance. Shoppers need to aim for more green and yellow labelled food products and fewer red ones in their shopping baskets.

Colour bars on front of products:
Red – high salt, sugar or fat content of food
Yellow – moderate salt, sugar or fat
Green – low salt, sugar or fat

Confusing choices

Some labelling systems can be confusing and over-complicated. Supermarkets and the food industry use parallel systems of labelling, making it difficult for shoppers to gather nutritional information at a glance. Critics also argue that they have been abused by the food industry. They claim that food producers have not provided clear, consistent and truthful information about their products.

Colourful labelling and 'healthy' claims on food in supermarkets can make it hard for shoppers to find nutritional information about what they are buying.

'If manufacturers choose to produce their own labelling guidance, it will only serve to confuse shoppers. Voluntary food labelling will only work if manufacturers look at it from the view of the consumer, rather than suiting themselves.'
Douglas Smallwood, Diabetes UK, backs the traffic light system, saying it is the quickest and easiest way for consumers to know what their food contains.

Binge

While most overweight people gain weight slowly, through lack of exercise or poor food choices, binge-eaters or binge-drinkers can pile on weight over a short period of time. The reasons for someone developing these eating and drinking habits are often complex.

Binge eating

Binge eating is a form of eating disorder, like bulimia nervosa (see right). A binge eater has lost control of his or her eating habits and will eat a huge amount of food, often in a short period of time, until he or she feels uncomfortably full.

This can be a way of coping with feelings of unhappiness, stress, depression and low self-esteem.

Bulimia nervosa

Bulimia nervosa is an eating disorder in which a person has episodes of binge eating followed by purging. The short-term relief felt by eating is soon replaced by an overpowering urge to get rid of the food by vomiting or taking laxatives in order to prevent weight gain. Despite eating a large amount of food, a bulimic person's weight may remain relatively stable, since most of the food does not get digested.

Someone with Bulimia nervosa vomits after eating as a way of controlling their weight.

A binge eater eats not because they are hungry but for psychological reasons.

'Media influences on girls and the Western ideal of **beauty are equated to thinness**. Girls are constantly exposed to images of very thin women, a body shape that is not normal or healthy, and strive to obtain this shape.'

Dr Jennifer Jones, Princess Margaret Hospital, Toronto, Canada

Teenage binge drinking is now a bigger problem among girls than boys in countries such as the UK and the USA. Some experts believe there is a link between alcohol abuse and eating disorders, such as anorexia nervosa, which are most likely to develop among teenage girls.

Eating disorders

Eating disorders result from a complex and wide range of factors, including social, psychological and biological conditions. Many people feel under pressure to conform to unrealistic body shapes displayed by fashion models (see right). In some cases people can take control of their eating habits and sort themselves out. However, doctors and other health professionals can help by arranging counselling or therapy. Sometimes it may be necessary to use a treatment centre where more support is available to treat the condition and its causes.

Binge drinking

In a number of countries, the consumption of alcohol has increased dramatically recently. A great deal of attention has focused on the culture of 'binge drinking', particularly amongst the young. The health risks associated with this are well documented, including brain and liver damage and mental health issues. However, binge drinking can also lead to obesity.

Most alcoholic drinks are as high in calories as soft drinks. Drinking five pints of lager during an evening adds more than 1,100 calories to a person's daily intake – nearly half of a man's daily energy requirement. Five bottles of alcopops contain nearly 1,000 calories, nearly half a woman's daily energy requirement.

Chronic obesity

When someone becomes severely obese it can be very hard to treat them. A BMI of 40 or more is called morbid obesity and in this case doctors will consider medical treatment with either drugs or surgery.

Finding a fat buster

A huge amount of money is spent by drug companies on finding a treatment for obesity. There are a number of drugs that claim to limit its effects but doctors will only prescribe these drugs in extreme cases and they are not suitable for children. They carry the risk of side-effects such as high blood pressure, anxiety and restlessness. Drugs are not a 'cure' for obesity but can form part of a weight-loss programme, combined with changes in lifestyle and diet.

Left: People's ideas of what is obese are changing. Some experts say that the increase in obesity has been so rapid that a body shape that used to be considered 'overweight' by many people will start to be seen as 'normal'.

Below: Two maps showing how levels of obesity have soared in the USA between 1991 and 2006.

☐	No data
☐	0 to 9.9%
☐	10 to 14.9%
■	15 to 19.9%

☐	20 to 24.9%
■	25 to 29.9%
■	Above 30%

1991

2004 – 2006 average

The drastic option

In the most extreme circumstances, surgery may be considered to treat obesity. One type of surgery affects the digestive process by shortening the length of the digestive tract. This means the amount of food absorbed by the body is reduced. In another type of surgery, called gastric banding, the surgeon places a band around the upper part of the obese person's stomach. This reduces the size of the stomach and so limits the amount of food someone can eat before feeling full. Combination operations reduce the size of the stomach and the amount of food absorbed during digestion.

Health risks

Surgery is not usually considered unless the obese person has made a major effort with other weight-loss techniques first. Surgical procedures, like drug treatment for obesity, carry risks. Operations are only successful if followed up by lifestyle changes. Patients must make lifelong changes to their diet if they are to keep the weight loss off in the long term. In the United States, obesity surgery is a rapidly increasing speciality, with over 100,000 procedures performed each year. Almost every private hospital, both large and small, performs the operations.

'To say there's underfunding of **obesity surgery**, is a massive understatement. It's appalling. There should be a public inquiry in my view.' **Professor John Baxter**, president of the British Obesity Surgery Society

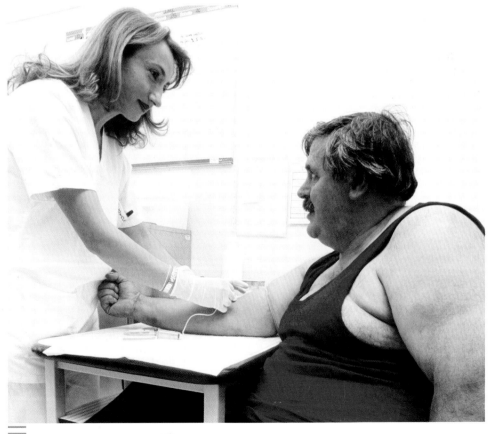

Losing weight and keeping it off is a long-term commitment. It is not easy, and it is important not to be disappointed with any minor increases along the way. It is better to look at the overall progress, and remember that any weight loss will improve health.

Obesity in education

Many people argue that schools are the places to begin changing young people's diet and exercise habits. They have the opportunity to offer healthy options during the lunch break that may also shape eating habits outside school. They can also endorse active lifestyles and teach a range of sports to suit all pupils.

Food education

In some countries, such as France, primary schools have begun to include lessons on nutrition and cookery. The same initiative is planned for secondary schools in England. Few children today learn how to cook from their parents. Health experts believe that practical cookery lessons and classroom teaching about nutrition are crucial in tackling future obesity. They also say that children should be taught how to understand food labelling and how to distinguish food advertising and marketing from fact.

Some schools encourage children to grow their own fruit and vegetables, which improves understanding of where food comes from.

'Their foods tend to be at **the bottom of the barrel** in terms of healthy nutrition.' **Dr Walter Willett**, Harvard School of Public Health, United States, commenting on the foods offered to US schools by the Department of Agriculture

These children are eating a typical school meal in London, UK.

THOUGHT BOX

How much nutritional information and cookery instruction do you receive at school? Do you think it is the school's or the parents' responsibility to teach cookery?

Sports such as football help children to stay fit and healthy.

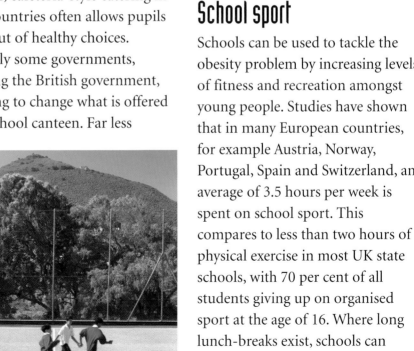

School meals

Controversy rages about the provision of school lunches in many countries. In France, small portions of adult-style meals continue to be cooked on site in most schools. However, cafeteria-style catering in many countries often allows pupils to opt out of healthy choices. Gradually some governments, including the British government, are trying to change what is offered at the school canteen. Far less fast-food is available than it once was. In Finland, schoolchildren are given no other option but a filling, healthy lunch. This includes a portion of salad but no dessert.

School sport

Schools can be used to tackle the obesity problem by increasing levels of fitness and recreation amongst young people. Studies have shown that in many European countries, for example Austria, Norway, Portugal, Spain and Switzerland, an average of 3.5 hours per week is spent on school sport. This compares to less than two hours of physical exercise in most UK state schools, with 70 per cent of all students giving up on organised sport at the age of 16. Where long lunch-breaks exist, schools can also encourage children to play more actively.

Eat well — live well

Some groups of people around the world lead remarkably healthy, long lives. When scientists investigate why, they usually find that it comes down to people living active lives and eating healthy daily diets.

THOUGHT BOX

Why do you think that so many healthy young women consider themselves to be overweight?

What is a healthy diet?

The bulk of a healthy diet should be made up of fruit, vegetables and carbohydrates (rice, pasta and bread – wholegrain wherever possible). People should aim for at least five portions of fruit and vegetables a day and try to avoid fried food as much as possible.

A daily intake of protein is also vital but this can be obtained from fish, eggs, pulses and nuts as well as meat. Calcium, present in dairy products and some dark leafy vegetables, is also vital throughout life for strong bones and teeth, especially during childhood.

Avoid special diets if you want to lose weight, and change your eating habits instead. Follow the food plate below to stay healthy and fit.

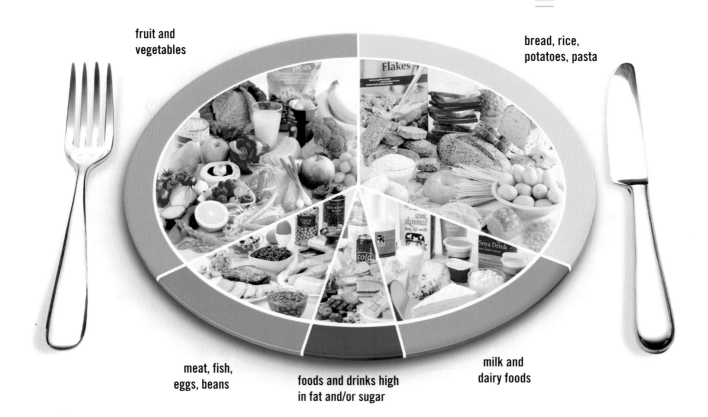

fruit and vegetables

bread, rice, potatoes, pasta

meat, fish, eggs, beans

foods and drinks high in fat and/or sugar

milk and dairy foods

'There's also a very important psychological issue. **Changing the food is only one part of it;** you've got to change the whole range of attitudes towards food too.' What 'attitudes towards food' do you think **Professor Ian Norton**, from The Formulation Engineering Research Centre at the University of Birmingham, UK, is referring to?

Increase exercise

The main causes of obesity are bad choices of diet and falling levels of exercise. The basic rule is: INCREASE the amount of exercise and DECREASE the amount of food consumed, especially foods high in fat and sugar. Walking to school or work, or getting off the bus a few stops before necessary, will help to boost physical activity as will walking for pleasure and taking up sport. If more people can put these lifestyle changes into practice, the global obesity crisis may begin to be challenged.

Healthy weight loss

People who are concerned about their weight should avoid special diets and slimming products. Rapid weight loss often leads to the 'yo-yo' effect, with the weight quickly regained, often with a bit more besides. The key is to change daily eating habits for the long term by choosing a healthy, balanced diet instead of cutting out particular food groups or skipping meals.

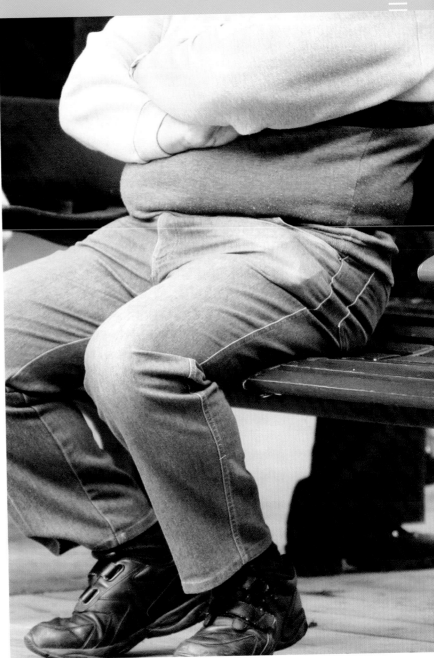

The key to losing weight is not to follow a special diet, but to eat sensibly and increase the amount of exercise you take.

The future

To prevent the worldwide obesity crisis that so many experts fear, changes need to be made by governments and individuals.

Health education

Some experts argue that health education campaigns, similar to those used to stop smoking, must target obesity. They should spell out the health risks associated with being overweight or obese. Nutritional and lifestyle patterns that are most likely to reduce weight must be encouraged and supported. The importance of physical activity in preventing obesity and reducing weight levels must be stressed.

Targeting childhood obesity is central to the fight against obesity. Schools must provide healthy school dinners, the opportunity to learn about nutrition and cookery, and encouragement for walking and physical activity. Other experts suggest that controls of the food industry need to be tightened. They say that laws should ensure a simple food labelling system that makes choosing healthy foods easy.

Drugs in the future

Scientific discoveries may be able to address the problem of obesity in the future. Scientists are trying to develop new drugs that lead to greater weight loss with fewer side-effects. One group of researchers has created mice with a faster metabolic rate. However much they eat, the mice stay lean, burning up the extra energy as heat rather than laying it down as excess fat. Might this one day be applied to humans?

Individual choices

Until there is a cure for obesity, most experts argue that each person is responsible for his or her own health and fitness. The causes of obesity are understood, as are the effects it has on a person's physical and mental health, as well as his or her ability to be fit and able to work. The key to success is putting everything we know into action.

THOUGHT BOX

How much fresh fruit and vegatables do you eat in one week?

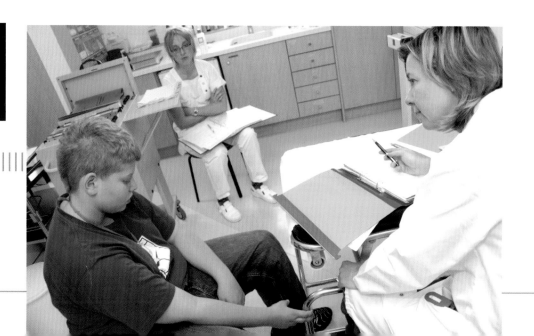

A dietitian in France sees a patient at a hospital specialising in obesity treatment.

'Multiple small changes in society have contributed to the changing population weights. We are going to have to intervene in multiple ways to push it back down again. There is not one simple answer.' **Professor Jane Wardle**, of the Health Behaviour Unit at University College London, UK

A huge amount of money is spent by drug companies on research to find a treatment for obesity.

Glossary

Additive A substance added to improve or preserve something.

Body Mass Index (BMI) A figure used to calculate a person's level of weight. It is calculated by dividing weight in kilograms by height in metres squared ($kg/m^{2)}$).

Bulimia nervosa An illness in which a person goes through bouts of overeating, followed by fasting or self-induced vomiting.

Calorie A unit of energy given by food.

Developed world The world's wealthy, industrialised countries.

Developing countries Countries that are less wealthy and less industrialised.

Digestive tract The organs through which food passes for digestion and elimination as waste.

Disorder A disruption of normal physical or mental functions.

Epidemic An outbreak of a disease that spreads more quickly and more extensively among a group of people than would normally be expected.

Genetics The study of heredity and the variation of inherited characteristics.

Kidney dialysis The process of filtering waste products of metabolism from the blood of a person whose kidneys are not functioning properly, using a dialysis machine.

Life expectancy The period that a person may expect to live.

Malnutrition A lack of healthy foods in the diet.

Metabolism The chemical processes in a living organism by which food is used for tissue growth or energy production.

Morbid obesity Extreme obesity.

Non-profit groups Charitable organisations.

Nutrient A substance that provides nourishment essential for life and growth.

Purging Ridding the body of food by using laxatives or inducing vomiting.

Quality of life A person's general sense of well-being.

Screening Testing carried out on a person in order to establish whether or not they have an illness or disease.

Sedentary Tending to sit down a lot; taking little physical exercise.

Self-esteem Confidence in your own merit as an individual.

Side-effect An undesirable secondary effect of a drug or other form of medical treatment.

Further information

Worldwide
www.who.int/topics/obesity/en
The World Health Organization is the coordinating authority for health within the United Nations. It is responsible for providing leadership on global health matters. This is the area of its site devoted to obesity.

www.preventionalliance.net
An organisation that supports new strategies to improve diet and activity and prevent obesity and its related diseases. Its special focus is preventing childhood obesity.

www.diabetes.com.au
The International Diabetes Institute.

North America
www.obesityinamerica.org
This site aims to help members of the US public, media and students get a grip on the huge topic of obesity. It focuses on the cause of obesity, its impact and research into how to reduce obesity.

www.nutrition.org
The American Society for Nutrition.

Europe
www.eufic.org
The European Food Information Council (EUFIC). This site contains science-based information on food safety and quality as well as health and nutrition advice.

www.foodinschools.org
A programme that aims to help schools improve food education and healthy eating.

www.bbc.co.uk/science/hottopics/obesity
The BBC's web pages on obesity.

www.nutrition.org.uk
This site provides healthy eating information, resources for schools, news items and recipes.

www.childrenfirst.nhs.uk/teens/health/healthy_eating
A website set up by Great Ormond Street Hospital, London, to help teenagers with lifestyle and diet. Includes a BMI calculator.

www.aso.org.uk
The Association for the Study of Obesity is one of the leading organisations in the UK on the treatment of obesity.

www.weightconcern.com
Weight Concern is a charity that is helping to fight the UK's obesity epidemic. It provides independent, reliable information on the health of overweight and obese people.

www.eatwell.gov.uk/healthissues/obesity
This site focuses on who is at risk of obesity and contains useful advice on diet.

Note to parents and teachers:
Every effort has been made by the Publishers to ensure that these websites are suitable for children, that they are of the highest educational value, and that they contain no inappropriate or offensive material. However, because of the nature of the Internet, it is impossible to guarantee that the contents of these sites will not be altered. We strongly advise that Internet access is supervised by a responsible adult.

Index